GOD COUNTS YOUR TEARS

"You have stored my tears in Your bottle and counted each of them." Psalm 56:8

Dr. Tope Ade

GOD COUNTS YOUR TEARS
Copyright © 2018 by **Dr. Tope Ade**
ISBN: 978-1-944652-74-6

Printed in the United States of America. All rights reserved solely by the publisher. This book or parts thereof may not be reproduced in any form, stored in a retrieval system, or transmitted in any form by any means - electronic, mechanical, photocopy. Unless otherwise noted, Bible quotations are taken from the Holy Bible, New King James Version. Copyright 1982 by Thomas Nelson, Inc., publishers. Used by permission.

Published By:
Cornerstone Publishing
A division of Cornerstone Creativity Group LLC
Info@thecornerstonepublishers.com
www.thecornerstonepublishers.com

Author's Information
Dr. Tope Ade
P. O. Box 5641, Frisco, Texas 75035
USA
Or Shalompcsc7@yahoo.com

The stories and examples used in this book are true but the names have been changed to protect the identity of the individuals

DEDICATION

This book is dedicated to my Lord Jesus Christ and to His Holy Spirit my Comforter and Friend. I also dedicate this book to the memory of my parents, Matilda & Joseph, my grandmother Felicia, my aunt Caroline and to everyone who has ever shed a tear or two.

To those who have given me the honor and privilege of walking them through periods of sorrow, grief, pain and joy; and have allowed me to see them at their most vulnerable moments.

ACKNOWLEDGMENTS

MY SPIRITUAL TEAM

…the Pastors, elders, spiritual leaders who stood by me, prayed with me, and visited me in the hospital and called me often – special thanks go to Pastor (Mrs.). Sanusi who called me often to ensure that I did not lose my mind, I also thank my mentor in ministry Pastor Toye Ademola

…the Kairos Team of Gateway Church Southlake Texas

…my Seminary Professors at Oral Roberts University College of Theology and Ministry, especially Dr. James Barber in whose class, Introduction to Pastoral Care and Counseling, I first realized my need for inner healing.

…My ministry partners.

…My prayer partners.

…My co-laborers in God's vineyard.

…The Wonderful Rejuvenate Team-Dr. Marcia Livingston, Edith, Pastor Victoria, Pastor Sade, Candi Young, Dr. McDonald, Ms. Dolapo, Dr. Bola…you guys are the best

...My protégées who believed in me and stood with me in my low Moments-Jibola, Edith, Pastor Victoria, Candi, Frances, Oyinlade, Dr. Samuel Ekundayo, thank you

MY FRIENDS

...I can't mention you all but cannot but acknowledge Larry & Maureen Sadiq, Rev. Merdis Buckley, Vanessa Griffin for spending nights with me in the hospital, Yemisi Bassey, Victoria A, Eniola A, Antonia King, Elsie....my friends on social media and many more, you all mean a lot to me

MY BIG SISTER

...Bimbo Ajayi M.D. what can I say? It's rare to see someone in their weakest moments and still respect the anointing of God on their lives. You saw and heard it all, but you never stopped believing in me, respecting and honoring the grace of God in my life. You remind me of David's mighty men

MY FAMILY

...Cousins, uncles, aunties – my siblings, Olumide Ph.D., Dapo, Tiwa, Eronse, Tunrayo Ph.D., thank you.

MY CHILDREN

...Eniami, Favor & Temmy. Ya'll rock! I love you.

AND YOU

...Yes, you reading this book!

CONTENTS

Dedication..7
Acknowledgments......................................8
Introduction...13

Chapter 1
Tears!...17

Chapter 2
Sowing In Tears..21

Chapter 3
Tears Of Sorrow.......................................31

Chapter 4
If God is so good…..................................73

Chapter 5
The Wounded Healer...............................87

Chapter 6
He Will Wipe Away All Tears...................97

An Invitation..107
About The Author..................................108

INTRODUCTION

Tears have always been associated with pain or distress but there is more to tears than just pain and distress. The idea of this book was conceived at a time of great distress and turmoil of the soul. Pain comes in different forms, shapes, times and seasons. My best form of communication is by writing. I found writing and journaling as a coping method to process my thoughts and meditate on God's Word. On this day when this book was written, the pain in my soul was so much that I felt it in my physical body. I lost my mother in 1992 and due to the sudden situation and circumstance that surrounded her death, I couldn't cry or mourn her. She was only ill for a couple of days so her death was sudden. There was no time to sit down and mourn as I had to take care of everyone around me because I am the oldest of her children. The relationship between my parents was strained before my mom's passing. She suffered emotional abuse, financial infidelity and some physical abuse from the only man she had ever loved and she became overwhelmed. I thought I had moved on, to suddenly find myself in what seemed like a vicious cycle. The man who was meant to protect me also began to abuse me physically, financially and emotionally.

The pain of 25 years after losing Matilda coupled with the current pain of going through a divorce all seemed to have overwhelmed my soul. The tears that had been bottled up for 25 years suddenly came flowing endlessly. On the eve of the 25th anniversary of my mom's passing, I began to ask God questions. God why have you allowed so much pain to ravage the soul of just one person? God why? As the hot tears were flowing almost blinding my eyes, drenching my pillows and comforting myself in the Lord, the Holy Spirit began to minister to me and I wrote down my thoughts in what came to become this book. In the course of my pastoral ministry, I have walked people through pain; some mourning either the loss of a spouse, parent, child, sibling, friend, family member, pet, relationship, health, property or job and being in so much anguish and pain. In processing my own pain, I asked God why He allowed so much pain in this world. Then I reminded myself that we are in a broken world with an assurance that those tears are not in vain because each tear is been counted by God.

One Scripture that ministers so much to me is found in Psalm 34:18, "The LORD is near to the brokenhearted and saves those who are crushed in spirit." The Contemporary English Version says, "The LORD is there to rescue all who are discouraged and have given up hope."

Another important thing to note is that Jesus Christ our Savior and Lord is described as a "Man of sorrows, acquainted with grief" (Isaiah 53:3). It is encouraging to know that in whatever season of life we are, our Savior can identify with us.

My prayer is that as you read this book, the Holy Spirit will comfort you and help you to find answers to your questions. God sees your tears, counts your tears and your tears matter to Him and, one day, He will wipe away all tears from all eyes. I pray this book ministers to you and serves as a constant reminder for you that you are always in God's thought, in His heart and also in His Loving Arms.

Dr. Tope Ade, June 2018

CHAPTER 1

TEARS!

"You have kept record of my days of wandering; You stored my tears in Your bottle and counted each of them" (Psalms 56:8 CEV).

Tears! Tears! Tears! The wet salty liquid that flows from the eyes down to the cheek and moisten the face. It flows most often as a result of expressed emotions; joy, pain, sorrow, excitement, depression; and even sometimes as a result of irritants in the eye. The dictionary defines tears as a drop of clear salty liquid that is secreted by the lachrymal gland of the eye to lubricate the surface between the eyeball and eyelid to wash away irritants.

Growing up, I did not like to be around raw onions because they made my eyes watery and they still do. I also remember as a little child that when I was upset and would cry that the tears will flow down my cheeks, mixing up with some gloopy slimy snot which would eventually make its way down to my mouth and I will lick it with my tongue. Yuck!

According to the Journal of Psychology, tears are the body's valve for stress, sadness, grief, anxiety and frustration. It is a form of cleansing and a way to purge pent up emotions. Most people are uncomfortable around people shedding tears and some see it as a mark of weakness. In 2012, when my aunty passed away from a terminal illness, I was very upset and I cried quite a bit. For me at the time, it was a tear of sorrow, fear, and anxiety all at once. Sorrow because my mother's younger sister passed twenty years after my mum; fear and anxiety because I felt that my mom's generation was gradually passing on and I suddenly felt odd, alone and fearful. During that period, someone called because he heard that I was upset over the loss of my aunty and he reprimanded me for crying. He felt that as a Pastor and a Christian leader, I demonstrated a lack of faith by crying. I was livid but I exercised some self-control; I felt like screaming but I held my breath and calmly thanked the man for calling and hung up the phone.

Many men have suppressed their emotions for the fear of being called weak; they put up a macho front of faux-bravery and sometimes end up with depression, anger and rage. Some become insensitive to other people's pain because their hearts have become calloused from the inability to express their emotion when necessary. Real men shed tears! A man that sheds tears shows his tender side, which does not make him a weakling but brave; brave enough to own up to his emotion and the ability to express it as often as needed.

Our bodies have been created to have the capacity to cry. Although excessive crying could be a sign of some deeper issues like depression; but tears have been known to have some benefits.

1. Tears lubricate the eyes;

2. Tears remove irritants;

3. Tears reduce stress hormones;

4. Tears contain antibodies that fight pathogenic microbes.

Judith Orloff, MD writes that the body produces three kinds of tears; reflex, continuous and emotional. According to her, [1]reflex tears clear out irritants; continuous tears keep the eyes lubricated with lysozyme which functions as an anti-bacterial; emotional tears contain stress hormones which get excreted from the body while crying. Emotional tears can also stimulate the production of endorphins, the body's natural pain killer and feel-good hormones.

No matter the reason for the shedding of the tear, God counts them. Shakespeare calls them, "Heaven moving

---

1   Judith Orloff, MD. The Empath's Survival Guide: Life's Strategies for Sensitive People, 2017

pearls." I believe that just as the Lord says He counts the hair on our heads, He also counts every tear simply because He cares (Matthew 10:30).

CHAPTER 2

SOWING IN TEARS

"Those who sow in tears will reap with shouts of joy" (Psalms 126:5 BSB).

Sowing is a process of planting or scattering of seeds which often come with a high level of anxiety and expectation. It is an action word so it often comes with the exertion of some labor. Sowing is an essential process for reaping except in some unique and rare supernatural situations even then, life comes in cycles and the reaper must have scattered some seed somewhere.

While serving as a senior pastor of a growing church in Richmond/Rosenberg Texas, there were days I was frustrated at the pace of numerical growth. One Sunday morning after having prepared for a wonderful service and had prayed for a mighty move of God, I went into the sanctuary expectant but the worship hall was sparsely filled with people; then I went into the restroom to cry and I heard the Lord say, "Would you wipe your tears and go out there and preach." I felt sorry for myself but God didn't seem to care. I quickly wiped my face and went out of the restroom into the assembly hall back to my seat and was ready to preach. God moved as He promised but the number of people in the sanctuary was very low.

Another Sunday with less effort, the Sanctuary was packed full with people of diverse race and ethnicity and we were the minority and I wondered where all the people came from. I planted a church in the Richmond/Rosenberg area at a time nobody I knew wanted to live there. At that time, I lived in Sugar Land which was a neighboring city to Richmond/Rosenberg. Most of the people I knew lived in the Sugar Land area and some clearly told me they could never worship in Rich/Rose because it was not an affluent community and nothing seemed to be happening there. I remember clearly that a lady ignorantly told me that worshipping in a city like that was to her like going "down to Egypt."

The Church was situated in between 2 cities, Richmond and Rosenberg, Texas but the parish was usually referred to as the Church in Richmond. As of 2003, the combined population of both cities was approximately 35,000 with a demographic make-up of approximately 65% Caucasian, 54% Hispanic/Latino, 10% African-American, 3.5% Asian and 31% of other races. The median household income was $35,510 with the per capita income at $14,814. The Lord laid the burden of

Richmond on my heart a year before the church was planted, therefore I had been praying for the city for about a year before the Church plant occurred. I led a group of people to the city for social-evangelism and welfare especially in the area formerly called the "Mud Alley." Mud Alley was an area infested with recreational drugs and other social vices.

Jesus is not selected about whom He saves, He died for all. "For God so loved the world that He gave His only begotten Son, that whosoever believes in Him shall not perish, but have eternal life" (John 3:16). Jesus died for the rich and the poor; the young and the old; male and female. He died for all peoples.

Anyone who has been involved in a Church plant knows that there is a lot involved and a lot of sacrifice goes with it. As a pastor, you might have to play several roles to keep the Church plant going. The leased space was a 4,400-square foot building and there were several classrooms for the children's Church as well as offices. The happiest place in the building was the hallway to the classrooms because it was always well decorated; thanks to the combined creativity of my personal assistance and myself. Although my ex-husband had a fantastic career that paid quite well, I had to make do with the stipend the church was paying me at the time which was barely enough for my commute and other expenses but I was fulfilled because I was living in God's purpose for me.

One day, while decorating the hallway and cleaning the children's section, I became overwhelmed with everything and I burst into tears. My car was in need of repairs and I did not have the funds to pay for it. While working, I was weeping silently and talking to God in my heart. I never doubted my call to the ministry, especially as a woman but I am also human. I started the Church plant while nursing a thirteen-month-old baby, with another toddler to run after, while their dad was posted to the middle-east for work, as a senior network engineer. I was running as a grass-widow with a major responsibility of pastoral ministry which I never regretted. I share this as part of my experience and journey.

On this very day while shedding tears, cleaning and speaking to God in my heart, my phone rang and I had to go to the hospital to see someone who was sick and on admission. I left what I was doing, wiped my face and drove down to the hospital. On getting to the hospital to see the patient, my phone rang again, and a lady told me she had a check for me. At first I did not quite understand what she meant; Betty was a consistent member of the church and she was also very faithful in her giving to the church. She had sold some oil dividend she had in West Texas and felt led to give the money and she said, "Tope, I just sold this oil dividend and I will like you to have the money; not the church, but you. You work so hard to take care of everyone." I was stunned; was I dreaming? Nobody had never given me anything as a pastor at the time, I was the one rather doing the giving including setting up a food pantry and sometimes personal items. It was fifty dollars short of a thousand, but it met my need at the time. I shed tears after getting off the call at the faithfulness of God. It seemed so scary that God answered my silent prayer almost immediately. "I will answer them before they even call to me. While they are still talking about their needs, I will go ahead and answer their prayers" (Isaiah 65:24). God did count my tears on that day and He responded faster than I could imagine.

Richmond/Rosenberg was my mission field at the time. There were nights of praying in the building, asking the Lord to build up the city and cause it to blossom. There was another pastor and his wife who took me under their wing to mentor. They planted the first charismatic church in the city and the wife would visit me sometimes and we would pray over the city. My children attended their Christian school at the time and I became friends with their only daughter. One day while praying in the building, the Lord opened my eyes and I saw an object hanging midair with long hair to its waist. I was not asleep neither was I in a trance. The object spoke and said, it was the principality over the city and its assignment was to frustrate the work of God and weary ministers in the city. It was somewhat frightful but I continued in prayers over the city. My team and I continued to sow seeds of righteousness against all the resistance we met spiritually.

We would go to the apartments in the community and evangelize; many gave their lives to Christ during those visits but never attended the church. In the process, I learned that we win souls not because we want to fill our church pews but because we want to populate heaven. God surely knows how to reward, while we were populating the kingdom of God and encouraging the people to attend whatever church they were comfortable with (we had a list of churches in the community they could attend), God was sending His own to our church. Majority of the members of Daystar Worship Center walked in on their own without been invited and remained faithful.

Years after I had handed over the church and left the city, I went back to visit and was amazed at the rapid growth. The city of Richmond had become the fastest growing city in Houston; the development was alarming and intimidating. I ministered at a church in the city and was overwhelmed at the goodness of God. This young church had purchased a 50-acre property for their church building at a prime location in the city. At the time while I was pastoring in the city, other colleagues told me to move to a bigger city but the Lord would not permit me. I knew my assignment was to prepare the ground by sowing seeds of prayers, the word, evangelism and humanitarian work. Although I am no longer in that city, I have seen the reward of God's faithfulness to His word.

I have seen parents sow in tears over their wayward children in the place of prayer. Dale was a wayward teenager who was from a good Christian home. His parents were white-collared professionals with highly paid careers. They never lacked but Dale was never content with anything. He would pilfer at all times and run away from home for weeks unending. Dale's mom would pray endlessly for her son to come back home and be safe from harm. It took years of prayer and supplication and a lot of tears. One day, Dale walked to his mom and showed her his letter of admission into college and the mother thought it was a dream. Dale graduated from college and got a good job and advanced in his career. He became his mother's sweetheart and took good care of her at her old age. He became a Christian and started a family to the amazement of many. "Those who sow in tears will reap with shouts of joy. He who goes out weeping bearing a trail of seed, will surely return with shouts of joy, carrying sheaves of grain" (Ps. 126:5-6 BSB). Dale's mother returned with shouts of joy with her tears watering her seeds of prayers over her son. I pray for that wayward child to receive the light of the gospel and be restored and delivered from every form of bondage this day in Jesus' name.

SOWING SEEDS OF PRAYERS

"The effectual fervent prayer of a righteous man avails much" (James 5:16). Many have sown tears of prayers for the

revival of nations, cities, individuals etc. In 2011 while I was in the seminary, I got a report that my brother was very ill. He was flown from another city to see a specialist and at a point in time, he could no longer talk. He had a severe lung infection and high blood sugar. I was restless in class and I would walk to the hallway to talk to the doctor on the phone. One of the days, my professor held me and prayed over me because the agony was deep; I was several thousands of miles away from him and the prognosis was not too good and there was no one close by to encourage me. I would go into my crawlspace in the Prayer Tower and weep my eyes out crying out to the Lord for his deliverance. When I got back home, I went into my closet to hide, cry and pray. "I cried unto the LORD with my voice, and He heard me out of His holy hill" (Psalm 3:4). The Lord showed me His mercy and He heard me; He wiped away my tears and He confirmed His word in the life of my brother. Most of the things I asked for in the place of prayer on his behalf have been fulfilled by God and I know that He who began the good work in his life will complete it in Jesus' name.

Mr. John migrated to America without his family. Like any other country, America has its immigration laws and everyone who wants to reside here lawfully will follow the due process. At this time, Mr. John was hopeful that his family would join him but it did not happen as fast as he had thought. Mr. John's wife was a few weeks pregnant when he left his country for America so he had never set his eyes on his daughter. I watched this man hope and pray for his family to join him. Weeks rolled into months into years and nothing happened. One day I saw the men gather round this brother as he broke down in tears because the pain of separation from his family was becoming unbearable. We prayed, fasted, cried with him and believed God with him as a church family but the answer did not come as fast as we thought it would. One day God heard his supplication, and I watched with moist eyes, Mr. John weeping and holding his daughter for the first time in her life; it was tears of joy and relief. Every seed sown in the place of prayer over his family bore good fruit. "Call unto Me, when you are in trouble and I will show you great and mighty things which you know not of" (Jeremiah 33:3).

CHAPTER 3

TEARS OF SORROW

"He will swallow up death forever; and the Lord God will wipe away tears from all faces" (Isaiah 28:5).

According to statistics, one out of one person will die someday. Death is a necessary ending for all humanity, and those who do not believe in Jesus Christ will die a second death. No matter how aged our parents are, we never want them to go. Separation in the physical can be tough because we were created to be immortal beings until sin came in and the curse was placed on mankind. The Scripture said, that the last enemy that shall be defeated is death (1 Corinthians. 15:26). No matter how one paints the picture of eternity with Jesus, physical separation through death is always very difficult and it is not easily accepted.

The worst thing that could ever happen to any parent is to lose a child. For many that have been through it, the agony is indescribable. In Luke 7:11-17, the Bible recounts the story of a widow who lost her only son.

> *"Soon afterwards he went to a town called Nain, and his disciples and a large crowd went with him. 12 As he approached the gate of the town, a man who had died was being carried out. He was his mother's only son, and she was a widow; and with her was a large crowd from the town. 13 When the Lord saw her, he had compassion for her and said to her, "Do not weep." 14 Then he came forward and touched the bier, and the bearers stood still. And he said, "Young man, I say to you, rise!" 15 The dead man sat up and began to speak, and Jesus gave him to his mother. 16 Fear seized all of them; and they glorified God, saying, "A great prophet has risen among us!" and "God has looked favorably on his people!"*

This woman as described by Luke was dealing with multiple sorrow; she was a widow, which meant she had lost her spouse and then her only son died. Her only hope of existence was taken from her. Her tears were endless. She had probably wept over the loss of her husband and now she was weeping over the loss of her son. In the Jewish culture, a son was a mark of strength and honor. That which gave her honor and strength was suddenly snatched from her. But the Lord who is near to the broken hearted was close by and He, the Resurrection and the Life raised her son from the dead.

When my mother passed away, my grandmother experienced deep hurt that no words could soothe. For her, life ended the night my mother passed away and I watched my nana aged suddenly. She was gifted with a petite and youthful look and never looked her age but she suddenly grew old and started looking her age. She was 78 at the time my mother passed away, but she very well passed for 65. Most nights, she cried herself to sleep calling my mother's name. I couldn't bear to see her hurt that much, so whenever I visited with her, I would pretend that things were well with my siblings and I, and that we had adjusted well to her death. My mother was 50 when she died and her mother died two years after her.

As a pastor, I have had to walk people through their grief and the most agonizing had been knowing how to comfort those who had lost a child. My grandmother felt empty and a part of her soul died that night. For such situations, I had always asked the Holy Spirit for a special grace to say the right word that would comfort the hurting and most importantly, I had to travail for the parents in prayers asking the Holy Spirit to reach into the depth of their soul where no one could and bring His comfort, answer their questions and give them peace.

Sue had suffered several spontaneous abortions and the last one she experienced was very traumatic and she almost lost her life in the process. To her, every pregnancy was a person because an unborn child has a soul and though unformed, had life. Life begins at conception. "Before you were formed in your mother's womb…I knew you" (Jeremiah.1:5). She was attached to every life that was formed inside her and she named them all. One day, the Lord decided to surprise her. She was pregnant and did not know it until the third trimester. She did not show neither was she sick for a minute; she gave birth to a healthy baby girl and she wept for joy. I pray for you this season that although weeping may have endured for a night, your joy is coming in the morning. God will give you double for your trouble and will turn around your captivity this day in Jesus' name.

Naomi was a woman who had suffered great loss. She lost her husband and two sons in a foreign land. "Now Elimelek, Naomi's husband, died, and she was left with her two sons. They married Moabite women, one named Orpah and the other Ruth. After they had lived there about ten years, both Mahlon and Kilion also died, and Naomi was left without her two sons and her husband" (Ruth 1:3-5).

Her grief was so great that she called herself "Marah" because she was a woman of sorrow, full of bitterness. "Don't call me Naomi," she told them. "Call me Mara, because the Almighty has made my life very bitter. I went away full, but the Lord has brought me back empty. Why call me Naomi? The Lord has afflicted me; the Almighty has brought misfortune upon me" (Ruth 1:20-21).

Naomi had a covenant with the God of Abraham, she and her family went to Moab as economic refugees and in the place where they had gone to seek a better life, she lost her husband and her sons. What a calamity? Her pillar was gone. Her husband, her protector, the supplier of bread, her lover, the father of her children was snatched away just like that. How will she survive? She picked up herself like a woman always does and received strength so that she could be a mother to her sons. Thank God she had sons, not just one but two. They became her rock, her pillar, her hope for living. She didn't mind toiling so that they would be okay, believing that one day, the boys will become men who would cover her in her old age, and her pain of widowhood would be forgotten.

In the Jewish culture, just like many other cultures, male children were highly regarded than female children (the Creator sees both genders as equal and as His image and likeness Genesis 1:26-28, and He loves them equally). Sons were seen as the ones who would continue the legacy of the father (Genesis 15:2-4). The word son in the Hebrew language is "Ben" it comes from a root word "Benah" which means to build. Descendants or families were assumed to be built by sons. Sarai appealed to Abram to have intercourse with her maid, Hagar, in order to "build" a descendant through her. "Please, go in to my maid; perhaps I shall obtain children by her" (Genesis 16:2b). The word obtain here means "benah" which means to build. The daughters of Zelophehad were almost denied their father's property and their inheritance because they were females who were assumed not to have any rights to their father's land, but thank God for Moses who sought God in the midst of the chaos.

> *"And the LORD spoke to Moses, saying: 'The daughters of Zelophehad speak what is right; you shall surely give them a possession of inheritance among their father's brothers, and cause the inheritance of their father to pass to them"* (Numbers 27:6-7).

In some primitive cultures in Africa, a woman was not regarded to have had a child if she did not have a son. The naming ceremony of the male child came with more excitement and jubilation than that of the female.

According to the Talmud, a father was obliged to circumcise his son (Genesis 17:1-14); teach him the Torah (Deuteronomy 11:19); find him a wife (Gen. 24); and teach him a trade (Mark 6:3) Joseph, Jesus' foster father was a carpenter and he taught his "son" the trade. According to Dr. Nahum Kovalski a Jewish medical doctor who made Aliyah to Israel in 1991, "He who does not teach his son a trade teaches him to steal." Therefore, a male child was accorded great importance and honor.

Naomi did not just have one son but she had two sons, Mahlon and Chilion. She saw in her sons the husband she lost and indirectly looked up to them for succor.

Her boys became men and they got married to Moabites women., Ruth and Orpah. She was excited and looked forward to being a grandmother and holding her grandsons and granddaughters and probably even naming one of the grandsons after her husband, Elimelek. Then suddenly, both sons died. Not just one, but the two. Her hopes were dashed forever. She felt empty, robbed, stabbed, and naked. Her day turned to night, her world collapsed. Was that just a bad dream or was it for real? Her breasts on which the sons suckled suddenly became sore again, her womb suddenly began to ache again. The pain was unbearable for her. She wished she could just die in place of her sons. Why was she alive? What was the purpose of her living? Her soul became bitter and she hated her name Naomi which meant Pleasant. What was Pleasant about losing a husband and two sons? There's nothing pleasant about her situation but everything about her life signified bitterness.

"Do not call me Naomi; call me Mara, for the Almighty has dealt very bitterly with me" (Ruth 1:20). She looked at herself and felt the Lord was against her. "It grieves me very much for your sakes that the hand of the LORD has gone out against me" (Ruth 1:13).

Sometimes when people of God go through tragic situations, there is the feeling that God was angry and was unleashing His anger towards the sinner. Sometimes, other Christians would make matters worse and assume the person had sinned, or was out of the will of God and a portrait of a God who likes to cause pain, a Schadenfreude, a Sadist is painted. But the Scriptures say that the Lord is good and He delights in the prosperity of His servants, the New Living Translation says, "Great is the LORD, who delights in blessing His servant with peace" (Psalms 35:27).

But Naomi's story did not end there. God gave her a daughter in-law who refused to leave her side. She was no longer a daughter in-law but her daughter, the one who would cover her in her old age. The one who would make her smile again, the one who would make her hold a newborn to her bosom again and smell the freshness of a new life. Naomi found hope again. For anyone reading this book who feels empty like Naomi, I pray that the Lord will restore you and give you joy as He did for Naomi and your life will be built up again in Jesus' name. Your life's journey will not end in pain, there is a new chapter about to be opened for you. A new chapter of joy, refreshing, hope, peace and your dreams will come alive again. I smell the scent of a new dawn coming for you. Weeping has endured for a night, yes a long night, but joy comes in the morning. And I say to you prophetically, "Good Morning."

When my mother passed away, I was the only one with her the night she passed; and it was so sudden that I remained in shock for several years. I bottled up the grief of losing her untimely for several years. I could hardly shed any tear. Six months prior to her dying, I suffered a broken engagement. I was engaged to a guy and three weeks to the wedding, he called off the wedding. I saw my dad cry for the first time. He wailed and ran into his room when the news of my botched wedding was broken to him. He later came out to speak words of comfort to me. The guy was entangled in another relationship and did not know how to disentangle himself. The pain and humiliation was unbearable for my mom coupled with the stress she was going through in her own marriage. His mom, a top designer had travelled overseas to buy the fabrics and everything needed for the wedding gown. I chose the style and about nine months to the proposed wedding date, she no longer accepted any contract form her clients (high clientele where mainly high profiled) until after the wedding.

She took her time to design the wedding garment herself; because she fondly said it was going to be a special wedding. She was very fond of me at the time and unlike the traditional mother's in-law, she spoilt me and would welcome me with a kiss whenever I visited. She carefully threaded every sequin, stone, bead and pearl on each line of the delicate fabric. Everything was custom made, including the hats and dresses for the bridal party. It was going to be the last wedding in his own family and the first in mine so there seemed to be some extravagance on both sides. I had carefully selected the wedding cake and went to the cake designer several times in Ikoyi for updates.

When he called to announce the cancellation of the wedding, I seemed unperturbed although my aunt was very upset so also was his mom. His mother threatened to kidnap him and bring him back home. We had met in New Jersey but I had to go back to Nigeria to complete my undergraduate education. My mother acted strong and pretended that all was well with her. She hid her pain from me while I also hid mine from her. We both pretended all was well when all was not well; we were both hurting and could not bear to see each other cry so we put up some fake smiles. From her voice, I knew she had been crying but never saw the tears flow down her cheeks. She was told to act strong for my sake. Many people praised me for my strength and complimented my mother for having such a strong and beautiful daughter. One of my uncles, Uncle Sam spoke words of comfort and courage to me. He said, "How could anyone ever reject such a beautiful, intelligent, kind, godly and resourceful young lady like you? My dear, he's the loser because you are going places." From my observation, most Nigerian families do not know how to grieve together and express their emotions openly. People often identify a dry face during a time of loss with strength especially if the individual was directly affected. That in itself could be a sign of trauma or a state of shock.

On the day of the wedding, I could not bear to stay at home. I did not feel comfortable being around anyone,

I wanted to be alone. The reverend waited in the church to inform guests the wedding had been called off. I remember the day I summoned up the courage to distribute the attires to the bridal party, my face was wet with tears all through but I would quickly wipe my face and reapply some powder before getting out of the car to drop off the attires at every stop. Being a hybrid of two cultures, I have noticed a remarkable difference in how both cultures processed their grief. When families grieve together, they also tend to heal together.

The night my mother passed away seemed like a long night and a bad dream. I never believed my mother could ever die. She did not have many friends but was a very kind and generous woman. She had the gift of long-suffering, always made excuses for others. She was very beautiful, elegant and very trendy. She worked hard and helped my dad build up a strong business empire which eventually crumbled after her death. She was a go-getter and a lover of aesthetics and jewelries. She had a huge collection of gold and purses. I would watch her apply her Fashion fair foundation to her honey colored flawless face and tie her long wavy dark hair in a bun and spray her perfume. Her dressing table was laid with a variety of perfumes, from Chloe[2] to Lancôme[3]. She was a nurse, a mid-wife and a successful business woman who was a neat freak and an excellent cook. She was highly loved by people around her and always had a calm aura

2   Chloe was a French luxury perfume
3   Lancôme was a French luxury perfume

about her. She was religious and towards the later part of her life, began to seek God more intensely. She was very compassionate and righteous-righteousness comes with helping the less privileged and helpless.

It was a raw and gusty night on the Island of Victoria in Lagos by the Kuramo waters[4] not far from the Bar Beach[5]. Mum had not been feeling too well and was resting as her doctor had advised. I stayed in her room watching over her but had a gut feeling that something was going wrong. There was the tropical storm and the beach was over-flooding its bank and the streets became flooded. The temperature in the room suddenly dropped and it felt like winter. I had just given her a drink of complan[6] which she barely took and I suddenly became anxious. I knew instantly that something was wrong. Her feet were cold and even after robbing them with my hands and some vapor rub, they remained cold. Her lips and finger tips looked grey and cold. Then I screamed her name, "Matilda." Her eyes popped open and she kept staring at me. I had never seen anyone die but I knew my mom was gone. It was Tuesday, 9th of June 1992 at 7.20pm. She died ten days before her 51st birthday. I walked out of the house to the street of Kasumu

---

4   A Beach in Lagos Nigeria
5   The Bar Beach was a beach on the Atlantic Ocean along the shorelines of Lagos, situated in Victoria Island, Nigeria. The Bar Beach was the most popular beach in Nigeria.
6   A nutritional drink like the American brand, Ensure

Ekemode[7] without shoes and in my pajamas confused. I sang worship songs, I screamed, I yelled, I sang, I ran, I walked; then I went back inside to make phone calls. I called the doctor, and a couple of family members. It took almost four hours before the ambulance arrived with my uncle and some cousins, by then rigor mortis had set in. I resisted her being moved to the ambulance and told the drive she was asleep and didn't want to be bothered.

It felt like a bad dream but I couldn't cry. I was so deep in shock and I went around like a zombie making all the arrangement for her funeral. I consulted with the church, selected her favorite hymns, made the announcement to her alumni association etc. The Thursday before she died, I wanted to be sure about her salvation so I led her to Christ. She was joyful about the experience and told me how she would devote the rest of her life serving God and her desire to go into a fulltime prayer ministry. I prayed with her and helped her get dressed not knowing I would never have the opportunity again. The tears would not come but I felt lost, afraid and alone. Had God failed me? Why did He let my mother die? I had several questions but there was no answer. I thought I was His child and was also committed to His service, why did He allow the devil to win, I thought? I was angry at God for betraying me and I felt like a fool for trusting God. She was buried in the clothes she

---

7   A Street in Victoria Island, Lagos Nigeria

and her sister had ordered for my botched wedding and her coffin laid at the altar of the Church where I would have been wedded six months earlier; at the Archbishop Vining Memorial Anglican Church.

Oftentimes when hurts run deep, there is a sense of betrayal which could lead to self-pity and anguish. In Psalm 44:23-26, the sons of Korah wrote, "Awake! Why do You sleep, O Lord? Arise! Do not cast us off forever. Why do You hide Your face, and forget our affliction and our oppression? For our soul is bowed down to the dust; our body clings to the ground. Arise for our help, and redeem us for Your mercies' sake." When we go through pain or hard times, we feel God has suddenly abandoned us, we feel unworthy and the enemy tries to whisper to us that we are not good enough and that God does not care about us. The devil reminds us of how others who are not as committed to God are faring better making it seem like all the years of fellowship and commitment to God was a waste. I may not have an answer to why you are going through and why you have gone through so much pain, but I know He promised, "I will never leave you neither will I forsake you" (Hebrews 13:5).

> *"The LORD is close to the brokenhearted; He rescues those whose spirits are crushed" (Psalms 34:18).*

My grandmother died two years after my mum. She had lived with us for about twenty-three years and had to go back to her home after my mother died. She wanted to be close to us her grandchildren but some circumstances did not permit her to. I would visit her occasionally and her sorrow over her daughter, my mom, ripped my heart apart. I had gone to pay her a visit this day and planned to spend the Christmas with her. As soon as I arrived at her place before alighting from the car, I saw my aunty, my mom's half-sibling in front of the house who had just found out my nana had been ill for a couple of days with pneumonia, and was about to take her to the hospital. There was no ambulance at the time because she lived in the country side of Nigeria[8]. I rode at the backseat of the car with her head on my chest, and I felt the heat of her last breath on my neck as she expired. She was 80. Tears flowed endlessly from my eyes and it seemed uncontrollable.

My grandmother lived with us for many years and read the Bible to me as a child and taught me how to pray. She practically raised me and I was very close to her. I listened to her Bible stories and stories about my grandpa, her childhood, and others. I watched her arrange her things orderly; she was a neat freak and a healthy eater. She exercised daily, ate a lot of green vegetables, very lean meat and fish and would only drink water and a glass of Dubonnet Red wine. She was only ill once that I could remember; she had a painful cyst on her back that had to be lacerated. I seemed to have grown up around some

---

8   Nigeria - a former British Colony; a country in West Africa, rich in oil, natural gas and various miner al resources yet impoverished due to poor leadership.

people with OCD. Her bathroom was the cleanest in the house and she didn't allow the maids to clean it; she did the cleaning herself and it was always spick and span that you could eat your lunch there. I learned to wipe my bathtub clean and dry after every bath or shower just like her. She was a disciplinarian and firm follower of Jesus Christ. God comforted me after many years of her passing especially knowing that she is currently with her Savior whom she loved so dearly.

Several years ago, my children had a betta fish whom we named "Sparkie." Sparkie was the center of everything for a little while until one day, we found Sparkie dead. My children were upset and they made me bury the fish in the garden and hold a brief service for it; after all, I am a pastor and a fish was God's creation. On the Easter Sunday after Sparkie's death, my daughter sighed and said, "Sparkie is in heaven now." And her older brother responded by saying, "Jesus cooked it." That was hilarious, but my five-year old did not find it hilarious. She cried and was very upset about the whole thing. Another time, she saw me with a few strands of grey and she started crying. She said, "I'm only five and my momma is old." I was about to read to them before putting them to bed when the whole commotion started. I didn't know how to respond but her brother came to my rescue and told her that "mum was changing to a blonde." She was very content with the answer and she smiled. To her five-year old mind, having some strands of grey meant growing old and to her young mind, old people die. Children have different ways of processing things but they are humans with feelings.

> *"In those days Hezekiah became ill and was at the point of death. The prophet Isaiah son of Amoz went to him and said, "This is what the Lord says: Put your house in order, because you are going to die; you will not recover." Hezekiah turned his face to the wall and prayed to the Lord, "Remember, Lord, how I have walked before you faithfully and with wholehearted devotion and have done what is good in your eyes." And Hezekiah wept bitterly"* (2 Kings 20:1-3).

Hezekiah was terminally ill and was told that he would die. His situation was similar to someone who was given a bad medical report and was told had a few weeks to live. Hezekiah wept bitterly. He wept with anguish and a sorrowful heart lamenting before the Lord and reminding God of his labors. God heard and added years to his life. Not many people received a new lease of life like Hezekiah did. When Lou received the news from her doctor that her cancer was terminal and that she had few weeks to live, she wept bitterly and called on God to heal her. She lived a few weeks longer than the doctors predicted but she went home to be the Lord. God is sovereign. He extended Hezekiah's life but Lou did not get healed on this side of eternity.

Twenty years after my mother died, my mom's only full

sibling also passed after a terminal illness. Two months after, my 80-year-old dad also died in a fire accident. I had a dream that morning seeing my dad looking peaceful with a huge smile on his face. He was smiling at me but he didn't say a word. I felt awkward and called to speak to him. He had dementia but he knew my voice and seemed always excited to hear it. I was told he was asleep so I instructed his caregiver to prepare him some fish stew and ensured that he ate well. His face kept flashing through my mind that Saturday and I ached to hear his voice but they didn't want to disturb his siesta. I hosted a breakfast meeting that morning and it was a highly inspiring and anointed service with a lot of worship and intense intercession. I thought about my dad all day and then at 6.30pm central standard time, my phone rang and my brother called to tell me the house was on fire. I later learnt my dad died in the inferno because his side of the house was ravaged with flames before the firefighters came. I had a preaching engagement the next day which was a Sunday, I couldn't cancel and the Lord gave me the grace to preach and I went back home thereafter, shattered.

With him, I never seemed to stop crying. I cried at every provocation and my son became my personal guard. He hugged me at every opportunity and was always by my side. It was a very rough Christmas holiday because my dad passed 9 days before Christmas; my church family sent me flowers, and I got calls from friends all over the world but deep within me, I wished I could hug him and tell him I loved him and had forgiven him but he was gone forever. During my visit with him on his 80th birthday 3 months earlier, there were moments he didn't recognize who I was, he knew my name but did not recognize my face. He took me to his room and blessed me and thanked me for my kindness towards him and I thanked him for giving me the best of everything at the time he did.

Most nights after my dad passed, I would sing myself to sleep and some days, I was too busy to cry because I was busy with my doctoral program at the seminary and somedays in the middle of a class assignment, the tears would well up in my face uncontrollably. I knew the ministry of the Holy Spirit was real, but at that moment I did not feel His comfort. My ex-husband celebrated a milestone party six months after so I had a lot of guests in the house, I was having a major digestive issue and was getting ready for a major surgery, while writing doctoral papers and playing hostess to in-laws, taking care of my children etc. I was overwhelmed but God held me.

"Unless the LORD had been my help, my soul would have settled in silence" (Psalms. 94:17).

In April 2014, seventeen months after my dad passed, I decided to attend a Kairos meeting at the Gateway Church in Southlake Texas. It was a two-day teaching seminar organized by the Freedom Ministry. The facilitators shared their personal journey to freedom and healing, the worship was intense and the atmosphere was supercharged by the presence of the Holy Spirit. In one of the sessions the Lord took me back to when I was 4. I saw myself in a beautiful garden dressed in a beautiful flowery frock and a young handsome man was playing hide and seek with me in the garden. There were butterflies in the garden and there was also a pond in the midst of the garden. I was very happy and there was a lot of laughter. Then the Holy Spirit in that vision reminded me of the trauma I had suffered as a child when I saw my dad pushed my mom who was heavily pregnant at the time. She fell on her stomach and I did not see her for a couple of weeks. I went from a happy child to a quiet, timid and withdrawn child. I stopped talking for a while and I developed separation anxiety. The Lord took me to the root of my pain, rejection and anxieties during that Kairos service. I was seated by myself at the back of the sanctuary bathed in my own tears when the Lord took me back to the occurrence 41 years prior. At this time, I was also going through a lot of distress and abuse in my marriage and I was getting tired and weary.

Suddenly, I felt something snap and my daddy wounds was instantly healed. A love for my dad flooded my heart and the tears could not stop flowing. I was healed of the daddy wounds that seemed to have almost scarred my life for decades, the tears kept flowing, washing away the pain and the hurts. I felt a tenderness towards my dad and wished I could hug him just one more time. God heard me and an altar call was made. I walked to the altar, and a mature, elderly male pastor almost in his 70s was there waiting for me. He was tall and lanky, bearing the last physical impression of my dad (dad had lost a lot of weight due to dietary changes and his dementia). The pastor wrapped his arms around me, prayed in tongues over me and blessed me. The tears of joy kept flowing down my eyes. I knew I was free; and an inner strength came over me. I believe that the comforting arms of the Holy Spirit were wrapped around me through that man of God to soothe me and squeeze out every pain in my soul. I sobbed intermittently and I suddenly felt some peace. The kind of great calm you feel after a huge storm. I began to hear the words of affirmation my dad occasionally said about me to my mom. How he thought I was a special treasure and how he prayed and wished I married a man who would appreciate me and honor me. I wished he said that to my face and not in a whisper to my mother, but the Holy Spirit kept ringing those words into my ears. I suddenly began to see how special I was and still am to my natural dad and also to my heavenly Daddy.

Something inside me began to resist being abused, the voice began to tell me I was created for more, not to be dishonored but to be honored; not to be abused but to be cherished and valued. The Holy Spirit helped me to see how much of a treasure I am to my dad and my Father in Heaven; I became delivered from the orphan spirit, I began to walk in the glorious majesty of the King's daughter that I am. I learnt to say no to intimidation, oppression and humiliation; I began to learn to stand unashamed, with God being my glory and the lifter up of my head.

Two months after that encounter, I was slammed against the wooden bed frame and kicked on the floor by my ex-husband in the presence of our 12-year-old daughter, and while on the floor something in me told me I was meant for more and valuable. The incident led me to the hospital for about 3 weeks, I lost feelings on my right side; I couldn't use my right hand and I limped for months. I wept one night when a male nurse had to carry me to the bathroom. I felt like an invalid but after my discharge and healing, I wrote a letter to myself from my Daddy, God. My encounter at Kairos prepared me for what was to come; the healing I received from the daddy-wounds helped me to rise up against the storm and rejection that was to come from the church for being divorced as a pastor.

Jesus had many friends, among which were Mary, Martha and Lazarus their brother. One day, Lazarus became ill and Jesus heard that His friend Lazarus was ill, but He didn't go there immediately, He waited till he was dead. Not few hours dead but 4 days dead and stinking in the grave.

"So when Jesus came, He found that he had already been in the tomb four days. Now Bethany was near Jerusalem, about two miles away. And many of the Jews had joined the women around Martha and Mary, to comfort them concerning their brother. Now Martha, as soon as she heard that Jesus was coming, went and met Him, but Mary was sitting in the house. Now Martha said to Jesus, "Lord, if You had been here, my brother would not have died. But even now I know that whatever You ask of God, God will give you." Jesus said to her." "Your brother will rise again." Martha said to Him, "I know that he will rise again in the resurrection at the last day." Jesus said to her, "I am the resurrection and the life. He who believes in Me, though he may die, he shall live. And whoever lives and believes in Me shall never die. Do you believe this? She said to Him, "Yes, I believe that You are the Christ, the Son of God, who is to come to into the world" (John 11:17-27).

Mary and Martha just lost their brother, their only brother. In a patriarchal society like theirs, having a brother gave them some form of security because the Scriptures never gave an account of the marital status of the sisters. He was sort of a covering for them until they met Jesus. They watched him fall sick and thought it was probably just a fever or a mild flu that would heal after a couple of aspirin or some herbal remedy and rest, rather, it led to his death. Lazarus, the friend of Jesus, the brother of Mary and Martha was dead. Martha vented on Jesus, "If You had been here, my brother would not have died." That could be a form of saying, Jesus, where were you when we needed You the most? Why did You forsake us at our time of need? When Jesus told Martha, her brother would rise up again, she seemed to say, "Yes I heard You Lord, I know I will get to see Lazarus again in the sweet bye and bye, at the Resurrection. When Mary heard that Jesus was in town, she rose up to go and meet Jesus and fell at His feet weeping. Holding on to His feet in worship, despair and anguish, shouting "Lord, if You had been here, my brother would not have died" (John 11:32). Has it ever occurred to you that both sisters believed in the ability of Jesus to heal their brother but not in His ability to raise him up from the dead? They both believed in Jesus, He was their very good friend.

Everyone knows you with Jesus. The neighbors know you are a friend of Jesus; you talk about Him, brag on His ability, preach about Him, boast of His love for you and suddenly, it seemed that that same Jesus was not there when you needed Him the most.

> *"Therefore, when Jesus saw her weeping, and the Jews who came with her weeping, He groaned in the spirit and was troubled. And He said, "Where have you laid him?" They said to Him, "Lord, come and see." Jesus wept. Then the Jews said, "See how He loved him!" And some of them said, "Could not this Man, who opened the eyes of the blind also have kept this man from dying?" (John 11:33-37).*

Jesus wept! Jesus still weeps when He sees us weep and agonize in pain; He weeps when we doubt His ability; He weeps when people question your faith and commitment to Him and wonder why you are afflicted; He weeps because He is forever living to make intercession for us (Hebrews 7:25).

For we do not have a High Priest who cannot sympathize with our weaknesses, but was in all points tempted as we are, yet without sin" (Hebrews 4:15).

Linda's brother died suddenly. Unlike Lazarus who was ill, her brother had no chance to be ill although he had a genetic defect but they did not expect him to die suddenly. Linda agonized at the physical separation, she knew she would see her brother Jimmy again but not on this side of eternity. She remembered them growing up together, the joyful family moments as well as the not too joyful ones, the pranks he played, the sibling rivalries, his plans for the future, his potentials and much more and she became overcame with grief. Her tears seemed to flow forever.

Elizabeth lost her older sister in a car wreck and nothing seemed to be able to comfort her. She wept for many months and went into a deep depression. Her husband did everything he could to help her heal but she remained in her place of grief. Prayers were said for Elizabeth that the Holy Spirit would help her to heal and wipe away her unending tears. One night she had a dream and she saw her late sister in the dream looking very happy and healthy, comforting her and telling her she was not dead but doing very well. She woke up from her dream and was comforted. Because the Holy Spirit is the Comforter, therefore He knows what can bring healing and comfort to every individual, He can use any means to communicate His comfort to us when we are broken.

THE TEARS OF JOB

The life of Job continues to be a story that never ceases to amaze me and it makes me to continually wonder at God's sovereignty. Job was a righteous man who loved God and took care of the poor and needy around him. He was very wealthy but he feared God and honored Him.

> *"There was a man in the land of Uz, whose name was Job; and that man was blameless and upright, and one who feared God and shunned evil. And seven sons and three daughters were born to him. Also, his possessions were seven thousand sheep, three thousand camels, five hundred yoke of oxen, five hundred female donkeys, and a very large household, so that this man was the greatest of all the people of the East. And his sons would go and feast in their houses, each on his appointed day, and would send and invite three sisters to eat and drink with them. So it was, when the days of feasting had run their course, that Job would send and sanctify them, and he would rise*

early in the morning and offer burnt offerings according to the number of them all. For Job said, "It may be that my sons have sinned and cursed God in their hearts." Thus Job did regularly" (Job 1:1-5).

This man called Job was the picture of a perfect man. He feared God, was very wealthy and rich, was an intercessor and a very kind man. Okay God, what else would You require from anyone? This man would rise up early in the morning to intercede for all his children naming them one by one. He was the envy of the people the cynosure of all eyes. Everyone in the East aimed to be like Mr. Job, he had it all. His life was perfect and faultless.

Then one day, his world came crumbling. Lucifer had been watching but could do nothing because the Lord did not permit him to afflict Job. The devil, the accuser of the brethren, had his eyes on Job. His accusation was that Job loved God because of the things God had given him.

> *'Does Job fear God for nothing? Have You not made a hedge around him, around his household, and around all that he has on every side? You have blessed the work of his hands, and his possessions have increased in the land. But now, stretch our Your hand and touch all that he has, and he will surely curse You to Your face!" (Job 1:9-11).*

The devil is the accuser of the brethren.

"Then I heard a loud voice saying in heaven, "Now

salvation, and strength, and the kingdom of our God, and the power of His Christ have come, for the accuser of our brethren, who accused them before our God day and night, has been cast down. And they overcame him by the blood of the Lamb and by the word of their testimony, and they did not love their lives to the death" (Revelation 12:10-11).

The devil is a thief. He likes to destabilize every stable life, home, nation and community. But according to John in the Book of Revelation, we overcome the devil by the Blood of the Lamb and by the word of our testimony. I speak over you this day that you are an overcomer, a victor and not a victim, a wonder and not a wanderer in Jesus' name. God's shield of protection over your life and family will not be lifted. This very day, the Blood of Jesus speaks mercy, deliverance, victory and protection over you and all that is yours in Jesus' name. Every accusation of the enemy is silenced by the Blood of Jesus. Then the Lord gave Lucifer the permission to afflict Job. "And the LORD said to Satan, "Behold, all that he has in your power; only do not lay a hand on his person" (Job 1:12). Yes, you read right, God gave Satan/Lucifer the permission to afflict Job but he was not allowed to take his life. Satan destroyed everything that Job had including his children yet, God remained on His throne watching. He knew the end of the story because of His Omniscience.

From the Scriptures and from my walk with God, I

have come to a conclusion that God is good and there is no evil in Him at all. God does not do evil. He is a good God and His mercies endure forever. "How God anointed Jesus of Nazareth with the Holy Spirit and with power, who went about doing good and healing all who were oppressed by the devil, for God was with Him" (Acts 10:38). God's goodness is seen all over even if the devil seemed to have clouded our judgment with our pain and tears. Job questioned God deeply at the time of his anguish. Who wouldn't? Job not only lost everything but he was afflicted with a skin disease. Out of pity, his wife felt he was better for him to be dead than to remain in the humiliation he suffered. His friends accused him of wickedness and evil (Job 22). Sometimes, when a Christian is going through a hard season, fellow Christians bring judgment and some even avoid the person like a plague.

I remember the year that I lost my aunty and a week after I returned from her funeral, my dad also passed away. A colleague in the ministry who was excited to be associated with me suddenly began to avoid me like a plague. It even became worse after my divorce, some ministers who knew the pain I went through and how I almost lost my mind in the process felt I should have remained married for the sake of the ministry. One of them clearly told me he would not feel comfortable inviting me to his church again due to his denomination's stand on divorce. I did not want to end up dying early like my mother and leaving her children in pain and agony. Many women and even some men have died in abusive and oppressive marriages because they are afraid of rejection. Some church leaders would rather speak at your funeral or visit you at a mental health facility, tied down and doped on medication than have you alive and in your right mind because they feel embarrassed that you have failed them.

Job began to question God in a manner that made him seem self-righteous. Remember, that no man can input righteousness on himself, only God can call us righteous. One day, God asked Job questions that revealed His omnipotence.

> *"Where were you when I laid the foundations of the earth? Tell Me, if you have understanding. Who determined its measurement, surely you know! Or who stretched the line upon it? To where were its foundations fastened? Or who laid its cornerstone, when the morning stars sang together, and all the sons of God shouted for joy.... Have you commanded the morning since your days began, and caused the dawn to know its place, that it might take hold of the ends of the earth and the wicked be shaken out of it?" (Job 38:4-12).*

God continued His discourse with Job, "Shall the one who contends with the Almighty correct Him? He who rebukes God, let him answer it" (Job 40:2).

"Our God is in heaven and He does whatever pleases

Him" (Psalms 115:3). God is sovereign! He is the Maker and Possessor of heaven and earth. He made the heaven His throne and the earth His footstool and He does whatever He likes in providence, in creation and in all things. He does according to His purpose and will not do according to our works but according to His good pleasure and only His counsel will stand. Because God operates outside of time and cannot be controlled by time, what we count as evil sometimes are in line with His divine purpose. "Thou art worthy O Lord, to receive glory honor and power; for thou art created, all things and for thy pleasure, they are and were created" (Revelations 4:11). God is the potter and we are the clay and are all works of His hand (Isaiah 64:8). One day I was in so much anguish and someone tried to minister to me using the life of Job and I told the person, "But I am not Job, I am Tope."

Several years ago, I asked the Lord to use my life for His glory. My heart cry was for my life to be consecrated to His purpose. I asked Him to use everything about my life for His purpose and His glory, I asked Him to sanctify my life so that it may please Him, then I wondered if I prayed amiss. Everything I went through did not look like my perception of God as a faith-filled believer. What happened to the positive confessions and the prayers of faith and the endless fasts, and prayers and offerings, and almsgiving, and supplications and services and commitments? Was God a figment of my imagination? Was He no longer in existence? Had He ceased to be God? Was the devil now stronger than Him? Did He escape to Jupiter? Why did He become so silent and cold? Was God a sadist? Why do others who do not serve you that much seem to have it all together? God, are you there? Can you please say something?

One day while in the administrative section of a hospital building to seek assistant for one of my church members, I fell ill and was wheeled from the administrative block to the Emergency Room. I was given some shots of morphine to put me out and was later placed on admission after the test revealed that my gall bladder was badly inflamed and was likely to be removed. When I came around and was able to use my phone, another church member had called wondering where I was, she had received a bad report from her doctor about the baby in her womb and she was helpless. I didn't tell her I was in the hospital until after I had prayed with her and believed God with her that the negative medical report would be reversed. True to God's word, months later, she had the baby and he was a picture perfect of health with no congenital defect. If God could use me to pray with others to get healed or receive their own miracles, why didn't He heal me?

One thing I have learned through all these is the process of trusting God wholly. If I truly believe that the Word I preach is true, then I must learn to trust Him with my life. Through this journey, I found out that the most difficult thing to do whenever you are going through a trial is to trust God. I found myself in a place of anxiety and fear because I thought God had abandoned me but that increased my anxiety and I was almost losing my mind and couldn't sleep. I would be driving and tears would be flowing down my cheeks that my vision would become blurry, so I would park in a safe place, sob and continued with my journey. Then one day, I was to minister at a church anniversary and the theme of the conference was "The Lord is my Shepherd." At first I thought, who in their right mind would chose such topic as their anniversary theme when there were more exciting topics to choose from. Then I began to study Psalm 23, and I found the message was more for me than the congregation I was called to preach to. From the study of Psalm 23, I discovered that God never promised us a trouble-free life, but that when we had to go through trials and tribulations, we would not have to do it alone for He would be with us.

A PSALM OF DAVID:

The Lord is my shepherd; I shall not want.

He makes me to lie down in green pastures,

He leads me beside the still waters.

He restores my soul.

He leads me in the paths of righteousness

For His name's sake.

Yea though I walk through the valley of the shadow of death,

I will fear no evil;

For Thou art with me;

Thy rod and Thy staff, they comfort me.

Thou preparest a table before me in the presence of mine enemies;

Thou anointeth my head with oil and my cup runneth over.

Surely, goodness and mercy shall follow me, all the days of my life;

And I shall dwell in the house of the LORD forever. Amen!

From studying Psalm 23 months before I preached on it, I learned that I shall always want. It is in man to always want and desire things and to love and to want to be loved; and, to always want to have our loved ones with us forever. I shall continue to miss my parents, my grandmom, my aunty, my half-brother, broken relationships, lost opportunities, lost resources, lost inheritance, lost times and much more. I shall continue to probe the empty spaces in my life but I will never feel deprived or be in want or feel diminished if I don't get my desires met because I know how blessed I am by what I have which can never be taken away from me. My Jesus! He is my all in all. He is my Lover, my Savior, my Lord, my Deliverer, my Provider, my Husband, my Teacher, my

Glory and the Lifter up of my head, my Joy, my Hope, my Rock, my Healer, my Comfort, my Yesterday, my Today and my Tomorrow. He is more than enough!

Then I realized my anxieties gradually began to go away. I started learning how to smile from the heart, I began to learn how to live one day at a time, sometimes not sure how the bills would be paid or how the children would fare but certain that He who sustains the world by the word of His power, was more than able to take care of me and heal me. I relinquished my will for His will; I began to pray more for those who had hurt me for them to be healed from their brokenness and be whole; I began to see God in everything; my compassion for the hurting and the broken increased; my sensitivity to the Holy Spirit kept growing. I began to guard my heart with all diligence not wanting to abhor bitterness or ill feeling towards anyone. I began to learn to say no when I needed to and my adolescents/adult children think an alien has taken over their mom. I began to crawl out of my shell to enjoy God's world.

I was bound by fear; fear of death, fear of being homeless, fear of abandonment, fear of tomorrow- then the Lord set me free. I began to trust His process even when it didn't make sense. I remembered my first encounter with Him when I was about 5 and was in a shell after a traumatic incident and I would only play with my dolls and no one else; and a man would come into our room and stand in a corner with a sword. He appeared huge but His appearance never intimidated me but brought me peace. I recollect telling my grandma about this person the first time I saw him and everyone thought I had eaten too much the previous night. How afterwards, I began to desire the word of God and my mother bought me my first Children's Golden Bible. Then I would sometimes hear an audible voice and someone tapping me on the shoulder while asleep and giving me Bible passages to read and several other things. Then I knew that the Lord was indeed near the broken hearted. The Lord reminded me of several supernatural encounters I had had with Him from my youth; several deliverances from death, and I began to learn to let go of my will for His will. I began to trust Him with my life knowing that He can single me out of the 7.6 billion people on the earth.

> *"Are not five sparrows sold for two copper coins? And not one of them is forgotten before God. But the very hairs of your head are all numbered. Do not fear therefore, you are of more value than many sparrows" (Luke 12:6-7).*

I am amazed at God's wonders. I am amazed at how He uses my brokenness to bring healing to many. I am amazed at how He has given me the boldness to crawl out of my shell and write my personal life journey. I remember one day my teenage children and I were discussing an issue and they said, "Do you think everyone is a turtle like you that likes to hide in its shell? We are social and not turtles like you." I am no longer a turtle but a soaring eagle. I am blessed that God could trust me with some of those life experiences and I am grateful that He held my hands and even carried me when I thought I could no longer stand. Paul said,

> *"But what things were gain to me, these I have counted loss for Christ. Yet indeed I also count all things loss for the excellence of the knowledge of Christ Jesus my Lord, for whom I have suffered the loss of all things, and count them as rubbish, that I may gain Christ and be found in Him not having my own righteousness, which is from the law, but that which is through faith in Christ, the righteousness which is from God by faith; that I may know Him and the power of His resurrection, and the fellowship of His sufferings, being conformed to His death, if by any means, I may attain to the resurrection from the dead" (Philippians 3:7-11).*

We need not underestimate any one's journey of faith; our stories defer, our paths to our destinations defer, our purpose defer, but God is constant. Sometimes others seem to have it easier, while some seem to have it rough; God is glorified through it all.

> *"Then Job answered the LORD and said: "I know that You can do everything, and that no purpose of Yours can be withheld from You" (Job 42:1-2).*

> *"And the LORD restored Job's losses when he had prayed for his friends. Indeed the LORD gave Job twice as much as he had before. Then all his brothers, all his sisters, and*

all those who had been his acquaintances before, came to him and ate food with him in his house; and they consoled him and comforted him for all the adversity that the LORD had brought upon him. Each one gave him a piece of silver and each a ring of gold. Now the LORD blessed the latter days of Job more than his beginning for he had fourteen thousand sheep, six thousand camels, one thousand yoke of oxen, and one thousand female donkeys. He also had seven sons and three daughters. And he called the name of the first Jemimah, the name of the second Keziah, and the name of the third Keren-Happuch. In all the land were found no women so beautiful as the daughters of Job; and their father gave them an inheritance among their brothers. After this Job lived one hundred and forty years, and saw his children and grandchildren for four generations. So Job died, old and full of days" (Job 42:10-17).

I love how God always turn around bad circumstances and make them into remarkable life experiences. Sometimes though, I still wonder why God had to allow Job to go through all that trauma. He could make the devil disappear or could have silence him; and He had the ability to protect Job and his family from the satanic assault. With my inquisitive mind, I have learned to gracefully accept the sovereignty of God and acknowledge that He is wiser than me.

"Oh, the depth of the riches both of the wisdom and knowledge of God! How unsearchable are His judgments

and His ways past finding out! For who has known the mind of the LORD? Or who has become His counselor?" (Romans 11:33-34).

I have also learned that,

"All things work together for good to those who love God and are the called according to His purpose. For whom He foreknew, He also predestined to be conformed to the image of His Son that He might be the firstborn among many brethren. Moreover whom He predestined, these He also called; whom He called, these He also justified; and whom he justified, these He also glorified" (Romans 8:28-30).

God has not forsaken you. His thoughts towards you are good thoughts and He is always mindful of you. His love for you is eternal and unchanging.

"Who shall separate us from the love of Christ? Shall tribulation, or distress, or persecution, or famine, or nakedness, or sword? As it is written: For Your sake we are killed all day long; we are accounted as sheep for the slaughter. Yet in all these things we are more than conquerors through Him who loved us. For I am persuaded that neither death nor life, nor angels nor principalities nor powers, nor things present nor things to come, nor height nor depth, nor any other created thing, shall be able to separate us from the love of God which is in Christ Jesus our Lord" (Romans 8:35-39).

Maddie was bent in shame and agony after she was raped

by someone her family had trusted for many years. This predator was a member of Maddie's parents' church with a brilliant career and a seemingly happy family, but inwardly, he was a pedophile and a child molester. Maddie was a member of the youth choir and a shy teenage girl. Her rapist, let's call him Jack, took special interest in Maddie and talked to her about her goals and gradually warmed his way into her life. He also eventually warmed his way into Maddie's parents' heart and being a "godly man" that they thought he was, they became friends with his family.

After the incident, Maddie felt dirty, rejected, ridiculed and worthless. She was a virgin and had never been with a man but this son of Lucifer decided to ruin another person's life with his own brokenness. As with many who have experienced sexual molestation of any kind or even rape, she loathed herself because she believed it was her fault. She cried herself to sleep and withdrew further into her own world. Like most who have been molested, she kept the incident to herself for almost three decades. She could not bear to tell anyone because she felt a sense of shame, guilt and abandonment. She starting cutting herself and found some relief in inflicting pain on herself. One day, the Holy Spirit invaded her space and overwhelmed her with God's love. She visited a Christian Counselor and shared her story for the first time. She felt like visiting her predator's grave and stomping on it (her predator died from a massive heart attack two years after violating her). She cried, sobbed, laughed, ached went through mixed emotions. Her healing was progressive, but she became better and stronger daily.

> *"God is our refuge and strength. A very present help in trouble. Therefore we will not fear. Even though the earth be removed, and though the mountains be carried into the midst of the sea: Though its waters roar and be troubled, though the mountains shake with its swelling. There is a river whose streams shall make glad the city of God, the holy place of the tabernacle of the Most High. God is in the midst of her, she shall not be moved; God shall help her, just at the break of dawn" (Psalm 46:1-5).*

For many men and women like Maddie out there who have shed tears of pain for being sexually violated, God is with you. He will help you and lift you up. God rejoices over you; you are not filthy because He cleanses you with His blood and covers you with His righteousness. You are valuable, because He redeemed you with His life. The Holy Spirit is bringing to life the virtues and gifts that were killed in you; He will make your heart tender again.

No matter what tears you have shed; tears of joy, tears of pain, tears of loss, tears of anguish and rejection or tears of anxiety; God counts them all. I believe that one day when we get to Heaven, Jesus will bring the bottle where He collects all the tears and show us how much He cared and still cares by counting every teardrop. The Lord is nearer to us than we know if only we can believe.

And one day, with His loving bruised hands, He will wipe away all tears from all eyes.

CHAPTER 4

IF GOD IS SO GOOD . . .

"For the LORD is good" *(Psalms 100:5)*

The question most people ask is: If God is so good why does he allow so much pain in the world?

One important thing we need to understand about God is that He is good. We do not deserve God's mercy yet we receive it daily. God did not have to make man; He is God and He can use anything to carry out His purpose. He created man because He is a relational God and everything about Him is love. He said,

> *"Let Us make man in Our image, according to Our likeness; let them have dominion over the fish of the sea, over the birds of the air, and over the cattle, over all the earth and over every creeping thing that creeps on the earth. So He created man in His own image; in the image of God He created him; male and female He created them. Then God blessed them, and God said to them, "Be*

fruitful and multiply; fill the earth and subdue it; have dominion over the fish of the sea, over the birds of the air, and over every living thing that moves on the earth" (Genesis 1:26-28).

God could have created other things to carry out His purpose, but He chose to make man in His image and likeness. To be created in God's image and likeness means the following:

1. We belong to God;

2. We are like God in intellectual ability, moral purity, spiritual nature, dominion over the earth, ability to make ethical choices, and immortality;[9]

3. We are made for God and for one another, made to love to be loved;

4. We are made stewards of the earth that God made, on which we have been placed. We are God's royal stewards; we are extensions of divine ruler-ship of planet earth;[10]

5. We are made to have dominion over the created order.

"What is man that You are mindful of him, and the son of man that You visit him? For You have made him a little lower than the angels (Elohim), and You have

---

9   Wayne Grudem, Systematic Theology, 1994, 443
10 Larry Hart, Systematic Theology, 233

crowned him with glory and honor. You have made him to have dominion over the works of Your hands; You have put all things under his feet" (Psalms. 8:4-6).

From this scripture, we can clearly say that God made man and placed him on the earth to represent Him. In the original context, it is written, "You have made him a little lower than Elohim." God made gods to deputize for Him.[11] We are the only creation of God that have the ability to make ethical choices. God instructs us but He does not force His will on us. "Choose you this day whom you will serve" (Joshua 24:15).

One day while travelling to the Valley of Texas for ministry, as we were close to landing, I had a great view of the city. It was gorgeous! There was the ocean on one side, then I saw some hills and later some low areas and the view was so beautiful and I wondered if an architect had designed it. God is the Master Architect that designed the earth. He designed the earth so that we, humans, can enjoy every bit of it.

God is self-existence. He does not need anything from humankind, He does not need any part of creation in to exist.

"God who made the world and everything in it, since He is Lord of heaven and earth, does not dwell in temples made with hands. Nor is He worshipped with men's hands, as though He needed anything, since He gives to all life,

---

11   Dr. Tope Ade, 2017

breath, and all things" (Acts 17:24-25).

God has existed before all things.

"Before the mountains were brought forth, or ever You had formed the earth and the world, even from everlasting to everlasting, You are God" (Psalms 90:2).

God created humankind for His glory (Isaiah 43:7); He also created humankind to bring Him joy (Isaiah 62:3-5; Zephaniah 3:17).

THE GOODNESS OF GOD

"For the Lord is good; His mercy is everlasting, and His truth endures to all generations" (Psalm 100:5).

One of the favorites sayings of one of my professors at the seminary was "God is good." Dr. Young was fond of talking about the goodness of God with much joy. Chancellor Oral Roberts' favorite saying was "Something good is going to happen to you because Jesus of Nazareth is coming your way." This song or saying of Oral Roberts is the truth because Luke wrote this in the Acts of the Apostles,

"How God anointed Jesus of Nazareth with the Holy Spirit and with power, who went about doing good and healing all who were oppressed by the devil, for God was with Him" (Acts 10:38).

When you hear of the goodness of God, I wonder

what comes to your mind. The goodness of God is His generosity.[12] Generosity is simply an act of kindness and liberality. It expresses the simple wish that others should have what they need to make them happy; it is the focal point of God's moral perfection. The good God of biblical revelation is neither a "Sugar Daddy" nor an austere, aloof judge. He is generous beyond our comprehension. He is a loving Father who delights to bless His creatures. Jesus taught: "If you then, who are evil, know how to give good gifts to your children, how much more will your Father in heaven give good things to those who ask Him!" (Matthew 7:11).[13] God is a good, good Father!

When Moses in Exodus asked to see God's glory; God chose to rather show Moses His goodness.

> *"And he said, "Please show me Your glory." The He said, "I will make My goodness pass before you, and I will proclaim the name of the LORD before you. I will be gracious to whom I will be gracious, and I will have compassion on whom I will have compassion" (Exodus 33:18-19).*

The word goodness in Greek is "agathos" which means to be upright, honorable, good, excellent, happy, pleasant or agreeable. Somebody once asked, "what is so good about the morning?" The response to this question

---

12   Karl Barth, Church Dogmatics (London: T & T. Clark, 1936)
13   Larry Hart, Truth Aflame

as that, "God spared your life to see a brand-new day, another opportunity to make things right and enjoy the beautiful world that He created one more time." The psalmist said, "This is the day that the Lord has made, we will rejoice and be glad in it" (Psalms 118:24). Another word used for goodness in Hebrew is "hesed." The word 'hesed' tells of God's commitment to being good. God is loyal in love. It is also translated as kindness, pure, gentleness, righteous and just.

The goodness of God is revealed in the wonders of creation. God did not create the universe and the earth that we live in because He had nothing to do. We can clearly testify that God created a masterpiece when He created the earth and we can never fully experience the beauty and wonders of creation in our lifetime because it is just too massive. God is liberal in His goodness toward humankind. Unlike man, God does not withhold His goodness from us even when we are undeserving. He causes the rain to fall on the just and the unjust. If I were God, I might try to teach someone a lesson and just withhold the air to prove that I have the power, but God does not need to display His show of power to prove that He is God. He is God and He is a good God. In Psalm 145, David celebrates the goodness of the God and blesses His name.

PSALM 145

I will extol You, my God, O King;
And I will bless Your name forever and ever.
Every day, I will bless You,
And I will praise Your name forever and ever.
Great is the LORD, and greatly to be praised;
And His greatness is unsearchable.
One generation shall praise Your works to another,
And shall declare Your mighty acts.
I will meditate on the glorious splendor of Your majesty,
And on Your wondrous works.
Men shall speak of the might of Your awesome acts,
And I will declare Your greatness.
They shall utter the memory of Your great goodness,
And shall sing of Your righteousness.
The LORD is gracious and full of compassion,
Slow to anger and great in mercy.
The LORD is good to all,
And His tender mercies are over all His works.
All Your works shall praise You, O LORD,
And Your saints shall bless You.
They shall speak of the glory of Your kingdom,

And talk of Your power,
To make known to the sons of men His mighty acts,
And the glorious majesty of His kingdom.
Your kingdom is an everlasting kingdom,
And Your dominion endures throughout all generations.
The LORD upholds all who fall,
And raises up all who are bowed down.
The eyes of all look expectantly to You,
And You give them their food in due season.
You open Your hand
And satisfy the desire of every living thing.
The LORD is righteous in all His ways,
Gracious in all His works.
The LORD is near to all who call upon Him,
To all who call upon Him in truth.
He will fulfill the desire of those who fear Him;
He also will hear their cry and save Him,
But all the wicked He will destroy.
My moth shall speak the praise of the LORD,
And all flesh shall bless His holy name forever and ever.

This is David, a man whose life was marked with varied life's experiences. His life was inspiring, exciting, and challenging. He lived in caves, deserts, valleys, the palace, and on the field as a shepherd boy. He was anointed King and chosen by God to rule His people yet He spent a great part of his life running away from his enemy, hiding in caves and feigning insanity. The drama in the life of David was exhilarating and at the same time agitating, yet, God called him a man after His own heart. He learned to trust God in the depths of depression, excessive danger and great rejoicing. He wrote that his tears were his food day and night and people continually asked him, "Where is your God" (Psalms 42:3). David's grief of feeling abandoned by God was intensified by the reproaches of his enemies, yet he wrote about the goodness of God.

In Psalm 22 David wrote, "My God, My God, why have You forsaken Me? Why are You so far from helping Me, and from the words of My groaning? O My God, I cry in the daytime, but You do not hear; and in the night season, and am not silent." The goes on in verse 3 to say this, "But You are Holy, enthroned in the praises of Israel."

What kind of person was David? How could he not curse God and walk away from the throne? Did he have to be king over Israel? David's knowledge of God was beyond the ordinary. He had an intimacy with God that was incomparable to none. Even in his pain, he talked about the goodness of God. How was he able to comprehend that? While running from one cave to the other hiding form Saul, he understood the mystery of God's divine providence. He understood that God was not the one who was trying to kill him but Saul. David understood that God will never, I repeat, never cause moral evil because He is full of goodness, but He permits it because He respects man's freedom and knows how to draw good out of evil. "God would never allow any evil if He could not cause good to emerge from it"—Saint Augustine.

God's goodness is revealed in Jesus Christ. His goodness drew us to repentance. Paul writes, "Don't you see how wonderfully kind, tolerant, and patient God is with you? Does this mean nothing to you? Can't you see that His kindness, is intended to turn you from your sin"? (Romans 2:4 NLT). His goodness led Him to taste death on our behalf. God is predictable. His predicted character is good.

> *"How God anointed Jesus of Nazareth with the Holy Spirit and with power, who went about doing good and healing all who were oppressed by the devil, for God was with Him" (Acts 10:38).*

DIVINE PROVIDENCE

Divine providence is the governance of God by which He, with wisdom and love, cares for and directs all things in the universe; animate and inanimate, seen and unseen, good and evil, towards a worthy purpose, because He is in control of all things. Divine providence does not destroy or hinder our freedom, rather, it takes our freedom into account and in the infinite wisdom of God, sets a course to fulfill God's will. God allows us to make our choices and still accomplish His will because of His power, knowledge and wisdom. He has numbered every hair on our heads, He knows about every bird that falls from the sky, and every thought and intent of our heart. God has the ability to bring good out of our bad decisions. Romans 9:13-24, Genesis 50:15-21.

I KNOW, GOD, BUT IT HURTS!

Twenty-five years after my mother passed, I literally mourned her for the first time. That same period, my divorce proceeding had started and I suddenly wished I could snuggle under the comfort of my mother. Few days prior to the 25th anniversary of her death, I locked myself up in my older daughter's room and wept profusely. I was curled up in a fetal position because the pain that shot across my body was indescribable. It felt like I was being run over by the wheels of a truck. I was badly in need of mama's hug or her soothing words of comfort but I found none. I thought I was going to go blind from the tears but I didn't. That period, I understood why some people mask their pain with alcohol and drugs. I had never drank nor smoked, but that period, I wished I could drink to mask my pain. Then I felt another level of compassion for people with drug and alcohol addiction; instead of judging them, I started praying for them. No wonder they drank so much! Most people with addiction do so to mask their pain; some are addicted to sex, food, alcohol or drugs, and use these destructive things to fill the vacuum in their hearts. I couldn't summon up the courage to drive to a liquor store to buy a bottle of alcohol or wine. While growing up, we occasionally had wine with some meals but it was the fruity sweet one and I did not like the way I felt afterwards so it was not my thing. Then I wondered how my children would have felt coming into the room to find me in a stupor dead drunk and wiped out, and wondered what legacy and image I would be portraying to them.

I remained in that condition for a couple of days, then I brought out my pen and started journaling. I wrote down the lessons the Holy Spirit was teaching me and also got a journaling Bible and started coloring. Thank God for my Divine Tranquilizer, He soothe me of the pain and I fell into a deep sleep. The Holy Spirit is truly the comforter. June 9th 2017 came and went and I arose from the potter's wheel a new creation. God does not delight in causing us pain neither does He want to break our spirits, the enemy does that already, but He uses our pain to shape and fashion us into something more beautiful and more functional for His purpose. One day after ministering to a woman who had just lost an adult son and was having a very rough day, she sent me a text that contained this message:

> *"The most beautiful people we have known are those who have known defeat, known suffering, known struggle, known loss, and have found their way out of the depths. These persons have an appreciation, a sensitivity, and an understanding of life that fills them with compassion, gentleness, and a deep loving concern. Beautiful people do not just happen."* – Dr. Elisabeth Kubler-Ross.

I felt so honored that God could trust me with such a painful process that could bring healing to many. Every birthday, I rededicate my life to God and the most recent one I had before the publishing of this book, I gladly and joyfully had another rededication ceremony in the privacy of my room to my God and King. I asked Him to take my life and let it be, consecrated Lord to Him.

When we allow the Lord to use everything about our lives for His glory and consciously seek the ministry of the Holy Spirit, rather than our hearts becoming calloused from pain, the Lord makes it tender for His glory. In the story of Jeremiah at the Potter's house, whenever the clay did not meet the approval of the potter, he smashed it down again into the wheel and remolds it. The purpose of the potter is not to destroy the clay, which is his work, but to fashion it into something more beautiful and purposeful (Jeremiah 18:1-6).

God is the Potter and we are the clay (Isaiah 45:9). God intentionally chose us before the foundation of the earth for His purpose. Our purpose in life is the expression of our personal significance to God and it is unique to us. God can choose to use anything to shape us for His glory. Through this process, we understand and appreciate the unlimited grace of God; we begin to come to a deep understanding of God - His glory and His divine nature; we also begin to discover ourselves and our purpose, and life begins to have some meaning and takes its shape.

David understood this hence he was able to write several songs about the goodness and the greatness of God. He sang, "For the LORD is good; His mercy is everlasting, and His truth endures to all generations" (Psalms 100:5). He also understood the mercies of God and He said:

"Bless the LORD, O my soul; and all that is within me, bless His holy name! Bless the LORD, O my soul, and forget not all His benefits: who forgives all your iniquities, who heals all your diseases, who redeems your life from destruction, who crowns you with lovingkindness and tender mercies, who satisfies your mouth with good things, so that your youth is renewed like the eagle's" (Psalms 103:1-5).

CHAPTER 5

THE WOUNDED HEALER

"And by His Stripes we are healed" (Isaiah 53:5d)

We live in a dislocated world, shattered and ruined by our quest for freedom. We want to be free from God and free from His laws. We think God must be a spoil-sport, trying to ruin our lives with the intention of making us miserable. Because He allows us to our free-will we attempt to hijack everything from Him and have ended up ruining the whole thing. Instead of seeking Him to help us, we look to ourselves and we end up causing more confusion and it becomes a vicious cycle. Life without Jesus is doomed!

ISAIAH 53:1-5

"Who has believed our report?

And to whom has the arm of the LORD been revealed?

For He shall grow up before Him as a tender plant,

And as a root out of dry ground.

He has no form or comeliness;

And when we see Him,

There is no beauty that we should desire Him.

He is despised and rejected by men,

A man of sorrows and acquainted with grief.

And we hid, as it were, our faces from Him;

He was despised, and we did not esteem Him.

Surely He has borne our griefs

And carried our sorrows;

Yet we esteemed Him stricken,

Smitten by God, and afflicted.

But He was wounded for our transgressions,

He was bruised for our iniquities;

The chastisement for our peace was upon Him,

And by His stripes we are healed"

When I first read this passage, I wondered why Jesus was called a man of sorrows, and acquainted with grief. In my young mind at the time, I thought Jesus must have been a very sad man, who walked around looking miserable by carrying the whole world on His shoulders-well He does carry the whole world in His hands, but with joy. No one can understand the pain of rejection like Jesus; no one can understand the pain of betrayal like Jesus; no one can understand the pain of infirmity like Jesus; no one can understand the pain of sin like Jesus; no one can understand the pain of death like Jesus; no one can understand the pain of humiliation like Jesus; no one can understand the pain of lack and homelessness like Jesus; no one can understand the pain of hunger like Jesus; no one can understand the pain of being lied against like Jesus; no one can understand the pain of loneliness like Jesus; no one can understand the pain of despair like Jesus. Jesus was indeed a man of sorrows used to pain and suffering. He didn't have to, but He chose to.

Jesus chose to leave the glory and splendor of His kingdom to come to the earth He created, marred with sin and pain.

"For we do not have a High Priest who cannot sympathize with our weaknesses, but was in all points tempted as we are, yet without sin" (Hebrews 4:15).

Jesus Christ our great High Priest and Mediator, never sinned, never yielded to the temptations, but was tempted and tested as we are; therefore, we have a High Priest who can identify with our weaknesses and the pain and agony that come with them. Jesus understands frustration, depression, hurts and feelings of abandonment. He is touched with the feelings of our infirmities and has experienced the range of emotions that goes along with feelings of hopelessness and uncertainty.

The writer of Hebrews describes our Savior in the days of His flesh, which means that while He was on the earth in His human form, He travailed in prayers, agonizing and making supplication to His Father to save Him from the gruesome death He was about to experience. The sorrow that overwhelmed our Savior was crippling. In the Garden of Gethsemane, Jesus in His distress said to His disciples, "My soul is exceedingly sorrowful, even to death. Stay here and watch with Me" (Matthew 26:38). Was Jesus saying here that He was so depressed and wished for death? Is the Savior trying to tell us that He understands the feelings of hopelessness and depression that brought suicidal thoughts?

Jesus was forsaken by His friends and He appealed to them three times to watch with Him but to no avail. The Scriptures say that "all the disciples forsook Him and fled" (Matthew 26:56). Have your friends forsaken you in your hard times? Rejoice! Jesus understands.

Sometimes, it could be a parent that would forsake their child. One of the deepest hurt that a person could feel is to have been abandoned by the parent. Several years ago, I met a young lady whose mother walked out of her life when she was a toddler. I got to play some role in her life and anytime she saw me, she would always want to snuggle close to me or wanted a hug. Something in her was crying out for the love of a mother that she was deprived from. I pointed her to Jesus; at the same time, we are called to be the incarnational presence of God to a lost and hurting world. We are relational beings and we thrive well in good and healthy relationships, so it hurts when the people you trust and feel safe with, abandon you, especially in a crisis moment. Jesus knew this, therefore, He sent us the Parákletos who stands by us as our Teacher, Advocate, Comforter, Guide, Enabler and Friend.

Jesus faced false accusation, was mocked, spat on, and struck in the face; given a hot slap! A slap in the face is humiliating, demeaning and dehumanizing. When we slap people in the face or get slapped in the face, the message we are communicating to them is that they are worthless. A slap is an act of violence although categorized as minor but its main purpose is to humiliate and shame. Jesus was humiliated, shamed and dehumanized just because of me.

"Then they spat in His face and beat Him with their fists; and others slapped Him" (Matthew. 26:67 NASB).

I loved my dad and I still love him although he's no more here, but he was sort of short fused. As a young girl, I had very dark, long, and curly hair and, my dad really liked it. It was braided, straightened with hot comb, put in a bun etc. and he was always ready to dole out the cash for my hair. He was a fantastic provider and the most generous man, except for Jesus, that I had ever known till time of writing. I did not like to ask for anything but my dad made sure he gave me what he thought I needed and wanted without me asking. He placed me on a generous allowance through my college years equivalent to the monthly salary of a civil servant at the time. I never asked, and I still do not know how to ask for help when I am in need except it has become overwhelming, but he gave me more than I needed. Our Father in Heaven does much more because He is a good Father.

At about the age of 7, my cousins who were living with us at the time were heading to boarding school and had to cut their hair. It was the norm in most Nigerian boarding schools for the girls to cut their hair especially in the freshman year, to avoid any distraction. I also asked to cut my hair and my mom obliged me. The following morning as I sat at the table for breakfast with my family, my dad sighted me with my cropped hair and his first reaction was to angrily throw his cup of water on my face. I felt ugly and shamed. For many years, I thought I was ugly even though my classmates would call me Ms. Pretty face but I never felt beautiful or pretty. I was shamed.

The face is the identity and it is the first contact people have with you. Many do everything to ensure the face looks good at all times; face-lifts, facials, or heavy makeup to hide flaws and contour the face. Our face most often reflects our inner condition of sadness, joy or pain. The face could show favor or dis-favor, the condition of the face shows acceptance or rejection. The face is crucial to our very being or existence. Show me a faceless person and I'll show you a person with no identity. Jesus had His face spat on, and He was slapped on the face. He bore our shame, became disfavored so that we can become accepted among the beloved. One day, not too far from now with the events unfolding around the world, He will be back for His church and we will behold His face and He will look lovingly into our eyes and say with a smile on His face, "welcome home."

> *"One thing I have desired of the LORD, that will I seek: That I may dwell in the house of the LORD all the days of my life. To behold the beauty of the LORD, and to inquire in His temple" (Psalms 27:4).*

The beauty of the LORD is the delight and pleasantness of His face.

> *"But we all, with open face beholding as in a glass the glory of the Lord, are changed into the same image from glory to glory, even as by the Spirit of the Lord" (2 Corinthians 3:18).*

> *"As for me, I will see Your face in righteousness; I shall be satisfied when I awake in Your likeness" (Psalms. 17:15).*

> *"Make Your face shine upon Your servant; save me for*

Your mercies' sake" (Psalms 16).

"For I will not hide My face from them anymore, for I shall have poured out My Spirit on the house of Israel, says the Lord GOD" (Ezekiel 39:29).

"Do not hide Your face from me in the day of my trouble; Incline Your ear to me; in the day that I call, answer me speedily" (Psalms 102: 2).

"The eyes of the LORD are on the righteous, and His ears are open to their cry" (Psalms 34:15).

"Do not hide Your face from me; do not turn Your servant away in anger; You have been my help; do not leave me nor forsake me, O God of my salvation" (Psalms 27: 9).

"With a little wrath I hid My face from you for a moment; but with everlasting kindness I will have mercy on you, says the LORD, your Redeemer" (Isaiah 54:8).

"The LORD bless you and keep you; The LORD make His face shine upon you, and be gracious to you; The LORD lift up His countenance upon you, and give you peace" (Numbers 6:24-26).

LORD, make my face loving and give me kind and tender eyes. Let my face bring peace to the hurting, and calm to the troubled soul. May my eyes never look down unto anyone with disdain; let my eyes speak of Your love to others everywhere I go. And may kind words proceed from my lips at all times in Jesus' name. The cry of my soul is to be just like You Lord. Many times, I want to be like Jesus, and sometimes I fail but when I realize my inadequacies, I cry out to Him to help me be more like Him; and, one day, I will be just like Him.

CHAPTER 6

HE WILL WIPE AWAY ALL TEARS

"And God will wipe away every tear from their eyes"
(Rev. 21:4)

The best thing that ever happened to the world is that Jesus Christ rose up from the dead and He is alive. His body was buried in dishonor but was raised up in glory. Jesus Christ is alive and well and He is interceding for us right now. And guess what? He is on His way back. One day, and very soon, He will split open the sky and take us home to be with Him.

Give me your tired, your poor, your huddled masses yearning to breathe free,

The wretched refuse of your teeming shore. Send these, the homeless, tempest-tossed to me;

I lift my lamp beside the golden door.

Our great nation, America was built by immigrants and

have thrived on immigrants. The early settlers were immigrants who invited other immigrants to come to the Land of the Free and Home of the Brave. To many immigrants, including myself, America is home. Many have fled from wars, economic hardship, banishment, terror and much more to the shores of America and have found solace, are thriving and enjoying the good of the land. As good as America is, it is far from perfect. There also thrives every kind of evil one can think of because it is not the perfect place.

We are pilgrims on earth, this world is not our home. No matter how comfortable we are on this side of eternity, it cannot compare with the glory and the splendor of heaven. Heaven is not a mythical place; it is a real place; the holy dwelling of God.

> *"But you have come to Mount Zion and to the city of the living God, the heavenly Jerusalem, to an innumerable company of angels, to the general assembly and church of the firstborn who are registered in heaven, to God the Judge of all, to the spirits of just men made perfect, to Jesus the Mediator of the new covenant, and to the blood of sprinkling that speaks better things than that of Abel" (Hebrews 12:22-24).*

> *"After these things I looked, and behold, a great multitude which no one could number, of all nations, tribes, peoples, and tongues, standing before the throne and before the Lamb, clothed with white robes, with branches in their*

hands, and crying out with a loud voice, saying, 'salvation belongs to our God who sits on the throne, and to the Lamb!' All the angels stood around the throne and the elders and the four living creatures, and fell on their faces before the throne and worshiped God, saying: 'Amen! Blessing and glory and wisdom, thanksgiving and honor and power and might, be to our God forever and ever. Amen" (Revelation 7:9-12).

"Then the temple of God was opened in heaven, and the ark of His covenant was seen in His temple. And there were lightnings, noises, thunderings, an earthquake, and great hail" (Revelations 11:19).

"Now I saw heaven opened, and behold, a white horse. And He who sat on him was called Faithful and True, and in righteousness He judges and makes war. His eyes were like a flame of fire, and on His head were many crowns. He had a name written that no one knew except Himself. He was clothed with a robe dipped in blood, and His name is called the Word of God. And the armies in heaven, clothed in fine linen, white and clean, followed Him on white horse" (Revelation 19:11-14).

"The twelve gates were twelve pearls; each individual gate was of one pearl. And the street of the city was pure gold, like transparent glass" (Revelation 21:21).

"In the middle of its street, and on either side of the river, was the tree of life, which bore twelve fruits, each tree yielding its fruit every month. The leaves of the tree

were for the healing of the nations" (Revelation 22:2).

"They shall see His face, and His name shall be on their foreheads. There shall be no night there: They need no lamp nor light of the sun, for the Lord God gives them light. And they shall reign forever and ever" (Revelation 22:5).

I have had two visions of heaven; the first time was in 1982. I had a dream that I died. Then suddenly, I found myself in a beautiful place. It had street lights and the light shining from them looked golden. The streets had golden color and everyone was happy and looked young. I remember that I saw little children riding their bicycle and everyone seemed so happy and peaceful. The streets were busy with people and they were chatting happily and cordially with each other. When I told my mom about the dream, she was frightened out of her bones because my dreams were very accurate as a child and she thought I was going to die. That year, I had a brush with death but God delivered me.

Another time I saw the vision of heaven was in Dallas Texas in early 1996. I used to go to the church building every Saturday to pray. It was a new Church plant of the Redeemed Christian Church of God and it was struggling like any new church plant. The worship team was quite interesting in those days, managed by in-experienced hands, mine, (along with playing other ministry roles), boy, we made a joyful noise to the Lord! I would go to the church to lay hands on the musical equipment because there was no one to play the drums or the keyboard; calling forth by faith, musicians, singers, volunteers etc. Declaring the things that be not as though they were and speaking mysteries onto the Lord concerning the mission. This day, I tried to pray but I couldn't utter any word, then I fell into a trance. I was by myself in the building. Suddenly, I saw myself on a speed boat crossing a river, then I appeared before a huge throne.

The throne was humongous and very bright. The light coming from the throne was blinding and I could not see the face of the person seated on the throne. The Light emanating from the Throne was indescribable and very pure that it went through whoever stood before it. The angels looked like lightening around the throne and kept chanting, "Holiness, holiness to the Lord. Holiness, holiness to the Lord! Holy! Holy! Holy! I couldn't utter a word but my mouth was ajar at the beauty and splendor of the place.

There was no dull moment there and it was loud and buzzing because there were tons of them (Angels). When I opened my eyes, I found myself on the floor of the sanctuary building and saw that I had drooled all over my blouse and it was wet. For several weeks after that, I felt a sense of calm and serenity all over me and I gradually began to drop off the cloak of religion and took on the mantle of God's love and grace. After that encounter, I stopped being religious, I gradually began to draw closer to the Cross rather than to the laws of men and my heart began to glow tenderly with the love of Jesus.

Jesus said,

> *"Let not your heart be troubled; you believe in God, believe also in Me. In My Father's house are many mansions, if it were not so, I would have told you. I go to prepare a place for you. And if I go and prepare a place for you, I will come again and receive you to Myself; that where I am, there you may be also" (John 14:1-4).*

Jesus was talking to His disciples about heaven and the invitation is extended to each and every one of us.

The only door to heaven is Jesus Christ. "I am the door. If anyone enters by Me, he will be saved, and will go in and out and find pasture" (John 10:9). Jesus is the only way to God.

> *"I am the way, the truth, and the life. No one comes to the Father except through Me" (John 14:6).*

I know you have wept and have perhaps shed several tears; one day, Jesus Christ will open His palms that were bruised with nails and lovingly wipe away all tears from all eyes. I believe He will show us the bottle in which He had been collecting our tears and say to us, "While you were crying and sobbing in pain and agony, My heart was hurting for you. I was right there beside you collecting your tears because they are treasures. While you were mourning, and crying over the loss of that loved one, I was there, counting and collecting your tears in My bottle. While you were tossing, and turning feeling restless and couldn't sleep because you were sad, I was there at your bedside, collecting your tears in My bottle. While you were shedding tears of joy for the relief you felt after much distress, I was there, counting the tears and collecting them in a bottle; while you were weeping because you were anxious and depressed, I was there right beside you, counting your tears and collecting them in My bottle.

Dear daughter and dear son, your tears were precious to Me; they reminded Me of My tears at the Tomb of Lazarus, in the Garden of Gethsemane; on the way to Golgotha and also at the Cross. Weep no more dearly beloved child, it's all over. The trials, the pains, the torments, the uncertainty, the losses, the hurts, the anxiety, the disappointments and rejection; they are over. Now you have Me with you forever" – Jesus Christ the King.

> *"Then one of the elders answered, saying to me, 'Who are these arrayed in white robes, and where did they come from?' And I said to him, 'Sir, you know.' So he said to me, 'These are the ones who come out of the great tribulation, and washed their robes and made them white in the blood of the Lamb. Therefore they are before the throne of God, and serve Him day and night in His temple. And He who sits on the throne will dwell*

among them. They shall neither hunger anymore nor thirst anymore; the sun shall not strike them, nor any heat; for the Lamb who is in the midst of the throne will shepherd them and lead them to the living fountains of waters. And God will wipe away every tear from their eyes" (Revelation 7:13-17).

That Scripture reminds me of a scenario one day as a little girl after sobbing because my mom travelled and I was anxious about been separated from her, my grandmother took me to the sink in the bathroom, turned on the tap and with her hands scooped the water from the tap and washed my face trying to comfort me that my mom was going to be back soon. Jesus is that fountain of Living Water.

Finally, "And God will wipe away every tear their eyes; there shall be no more death, nor sorrow, nor crying. There shall be no more pain, for the former things have passed away. Then He who sat on the throne said, 'Behold, I make all things new.' And He said to me, 'Write, for these words are true and faithful.' And He said to me, 'It is done! I am the Alpha and Omega, the Beginning and the End. I will give of the fountain of life freely to him who thirsts. He who overcomes shall inherit all things and I will be his God and he shall be My son" (Revelation 21:4-7).

Soon and very soon, we will see the King. Do not give up on life, you are an overcomer already. The fact that you are alive to read this book tells me that you will overcome because you believe that one day, Jesus Christ, our Savior, Lord and King, will wipe away those tears and give you a new name. Get out of that bed of depression, there is a purpose for your tears and pain. Somebody somewhere is counting on you, waiting to hear your story and ask how you overcame. Don't attempt that suicide, there is hope for you; God is not done with you yet, a new chapter is about to be opened and it's full of pleasant surprises. Weeping has endured for a long night, but your joy is here.

Good Morning!

AN INVITATION

Then Jesus said, "Come to Me, all you who are weary and carry heaven burdens, and I will give you rest. Take My yoke upon you. Let Me teach you, because I am humble and gentle at heart, and you will find rest for your souls" (Matthew. 11:28-29 NLT).

> *"Look! I stand at the door and knock. If you hear My voice and open the door, I will come in, and we will share a meal together as friends"* (Revelation 3:20).

Jesus is waiting to relieve you of your heavy burdens and He is knocking at the door of your heart. Would you let Him in? Would you surrender your life to The Savior today? He has been where you are and He wants to take you where He is.

If you surrendered your life to Jesus by reading this book, could you please do me a favor and share your story of salvation with me.

Contact:
Dr. Tope Ade
P. O. Box 5641, Frisco, Texas 75035
USA
Or Shalompcsc7@yahoo.com

ABOUT THE AUTHOR

Dr. Tope Ade had her early childhood in Lagos Nigeria, West Africa in an upper middle-class home. She was born to Matilda a Senior Registered Nurse and a Midwife who later became a business entrepreneur; and also to Joseph a Senior Commercial Manager with IBM and later ventured into business on his own along with his wife.

She attended a Catholic Convent Private School for her elementary education and also a Catholic High School for her secondary education. She obtained a Bachelor of Arts in Education from Lagos State University in Nigeria, in 1990. She had an encounter with the Lord at a very young age through the influence of her maternal grandmother, Felicia, who was a devoted Christian in the Anglican Communion. In June 1984, she formally accepted Jesus Christ as her Savior and Lord. Dr. Tope has been serving in the church since the age of 10 and was commissioned as a minister in 1996 and ordained in May 1997 in Tallahassee Florida under the apostolic leadership of Pastor E. A. Adeboye, Ph.D., the General Overseer of The Redeemed Christian Church of God worldwide. She has served in various roles as an Usher, Choir Member/Leader, Prayer Group Leader, Sunday School Teacher, Believers' Foundation Class Teacher,

Leader of the Workers' Directorate, Pastoral Care, Singles & Youth Leader, Church Janitor, Administrator, Associate Pastor and later as a Senior Parish Pastor. She served as the Lead Campus Pastor of Daystar Worship Center, Rosenberg Texas for about 7 years and left to complete her Seminary training at Oral Roberts University, College of Theology and Ministry, in Tulsa Oklahoma, and graduated with a Doctor of Ministry Degree with Concentration in Church Ministries and Leadership, as well as a Master of Divinity Degree from the same institution. She is also working on a Master of Arts in Human Services Counseling from Regent University, Virginia Beach, VA.

She worked in the Financial Services Industry and Investment Banking in Corporate America before going into full-time ministry.

Dr. Tope Ade is a Pastor, Teacher, Bible Scholar, Christian Life Coach, a Pastoral Counselor and a Mentor to many. Her heart desire is to see the Church of Jesus Christ, equipped with the Truth and walking in Freedom and wholeness, so as to be able to faithfully serve God through His people in a disjointed and dislocated world; being the Incarnational Presence of Jesus Christ. She is a prolific writer and author, a lover of nature with an artistic flair. She loves to cook, bake and entertain very intimate friends. She enjoys gardening, painting, drawing and traveling. She hopes to play the Grand Piano and the Guitar someday. She has two adult children, a teenager and a grandson, Josef. She loves Jesus passionately and keeps cultivating her relationship with the Holy Spirit. Pastor T, as fondly called by a few, keeps walking towards Jesus in freedom and healing from past hurts and pain. She is an intercessor and an intense worshipper.

She is the founder of Liberation Call Christian Ministries in Frisco Texas, the Director of Pneuma-logos Centre for Biblical Mentoring and Training, and Shalom Soul Care & Spiritual Formation Clinic. She is a visiting Professor/Scholar to some Bible institutes in Africa, a Church Planter and itinerant preacher. She holds an annual conference themed Rejuvenate for Women in Leadership, The Revive Transformational Conference, a teaching, prayer and healing revival meeting and other meetings. She travels all over the world to speak in churches, conferences and conventions, and also to train and equip church leaders and missionaries.

Dr. Tope's most favorite place is her home with her family, cooking, baking with her nieces, grocery shopping, gardening or locked up in her room reading. She hopes to adopt a Yorkie Terrier sometime soon, and looks forward to someday when she will lay her crowns before the feet of her Lover, Savior, Friend, Lord and Master, Jesus Christ.

"And God will wipe away every tear from their eyes; there shall be no more death, sorrow, nor crying. There shall be no more pain, for the former things have passed away."

Revelation 21:4 (NKJV)

www.ingramcontent.com/pod-product-compliance
Lightning Source LLC
Chambersburg PA
CBHW070648050426
42451CB00008B/313